THE ADULT COLOURING BOOK OF HILARIOUSLY FUNNY MOVIE QUOTES

R. J. Duncan

All of the quotes included in the book are the property of their rightful owners (Production Companies, Writers, Developers, etc.) and not a single piece of this work is meant to infringe on any copyrights.

All the designs for this book were made by a very talented artist, Francesco Virdis. Follow him on Instagram: **@virdis_art**

If you're not sure which movie some of the quotes are from, you can go to rjduncanbooks.com for a full list of movie titles and actors that portrayed the characters.

I truly hope you enjoy this book.

Dig in!

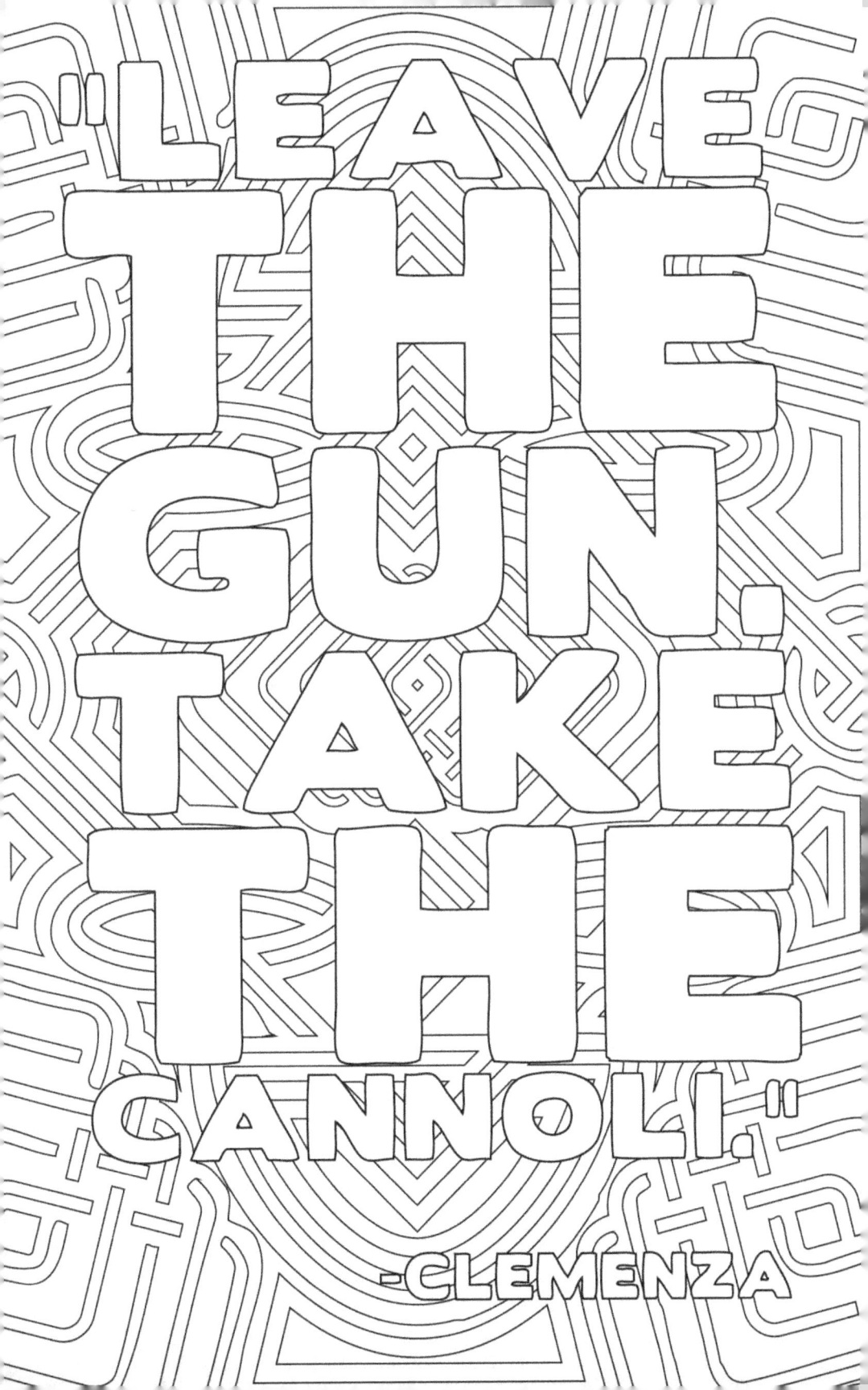

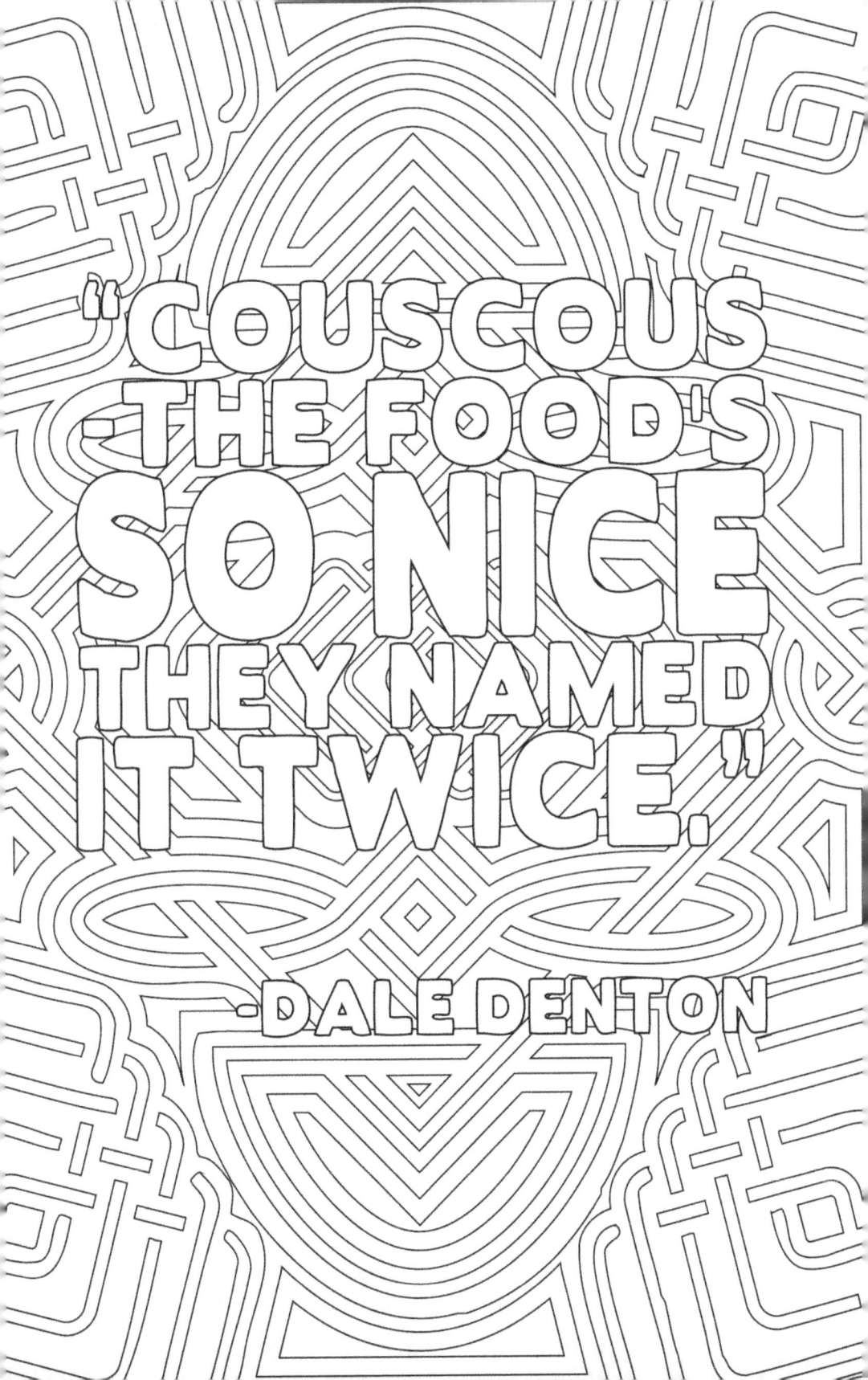

"C'MON, RHYTHM! HUT, 2, 3, 4. BLACK GUYS, HELP THE WHITE GUYS."

-RUSSELL ZISKEY

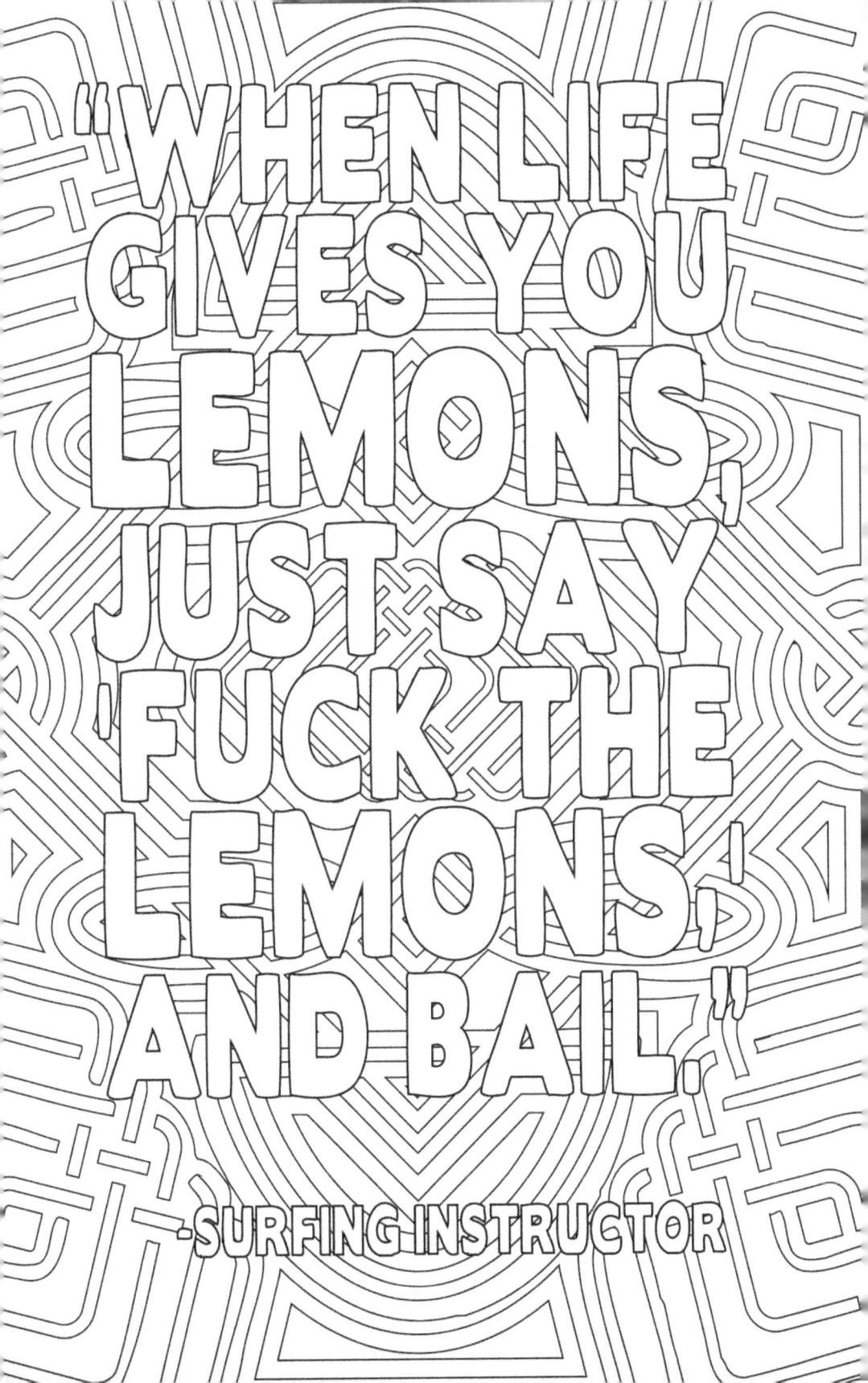

"ME AND THE JUDGE HAVE A SPECIAL RELATIONSHIP... I DON'T WANNA GET TOO GRAPHIC BUT I SUCKED HIS DICK FOR DRUGS."

-GAYLE SWEENY

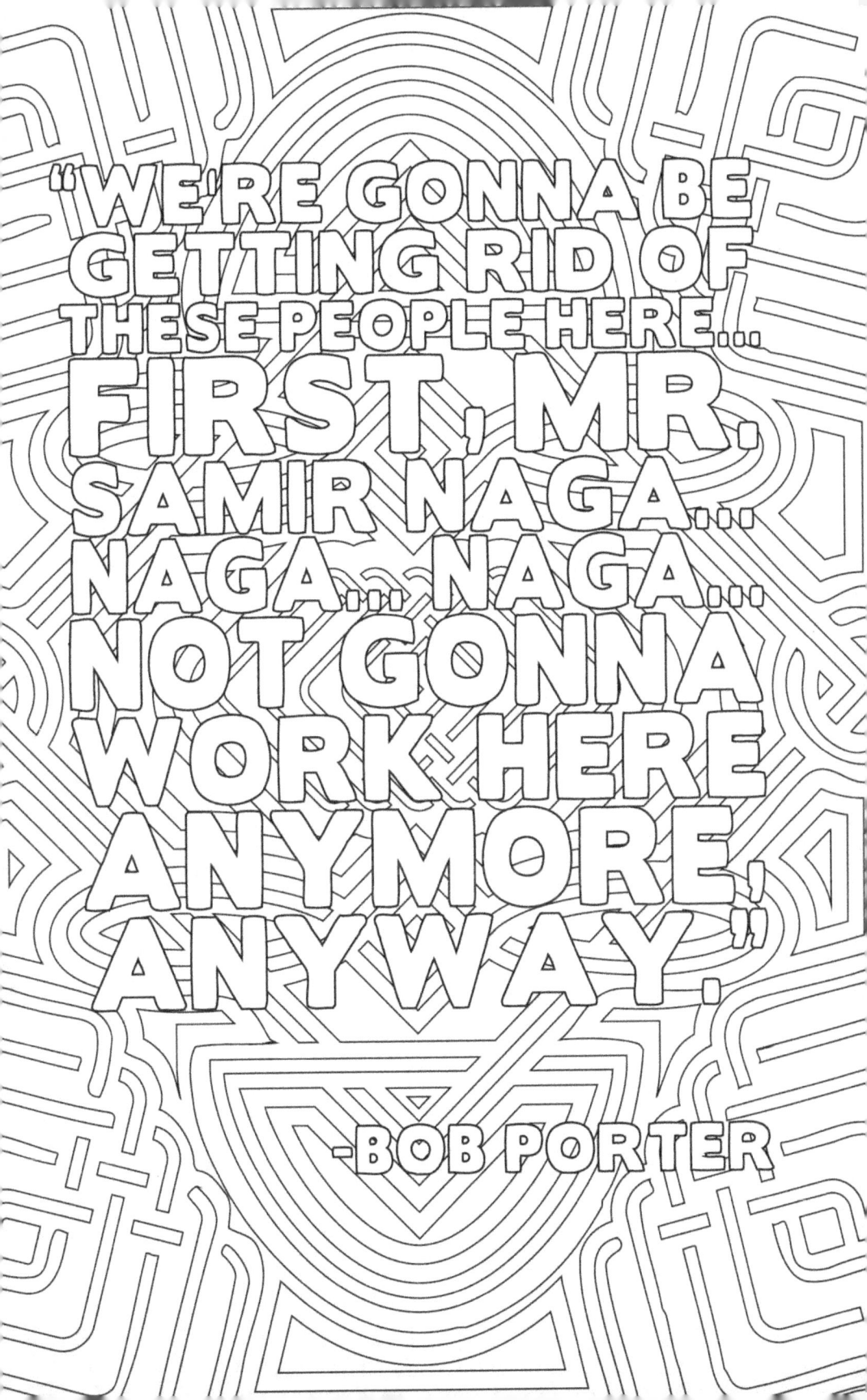

"OH, BUT YOU CAN'T EXPECT TO WIELD SUPREME EXECUTIVE POWER JUST BECAUSE SOME WATERY TART THREW A SWORD AT YOU."

-DENNIS

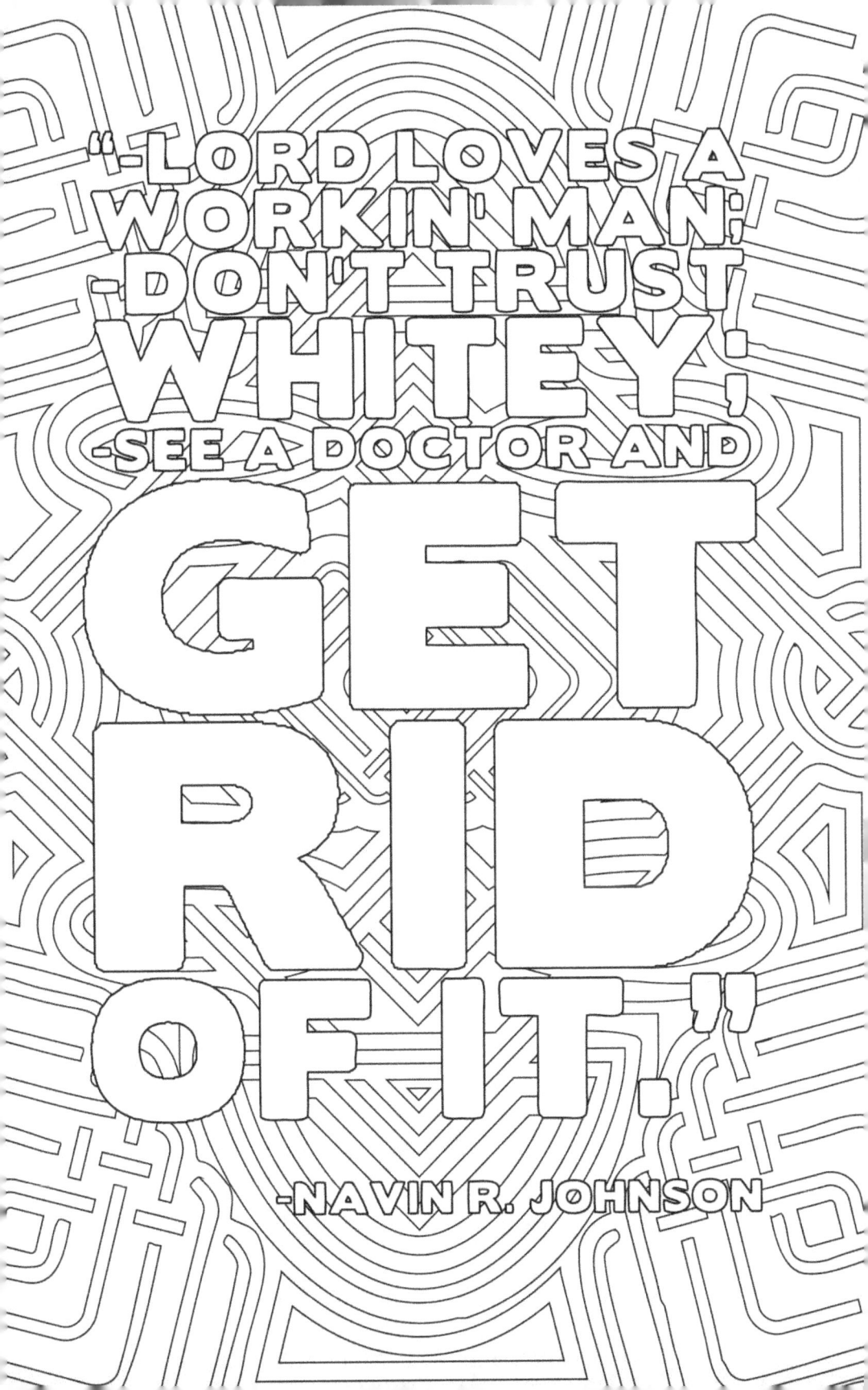

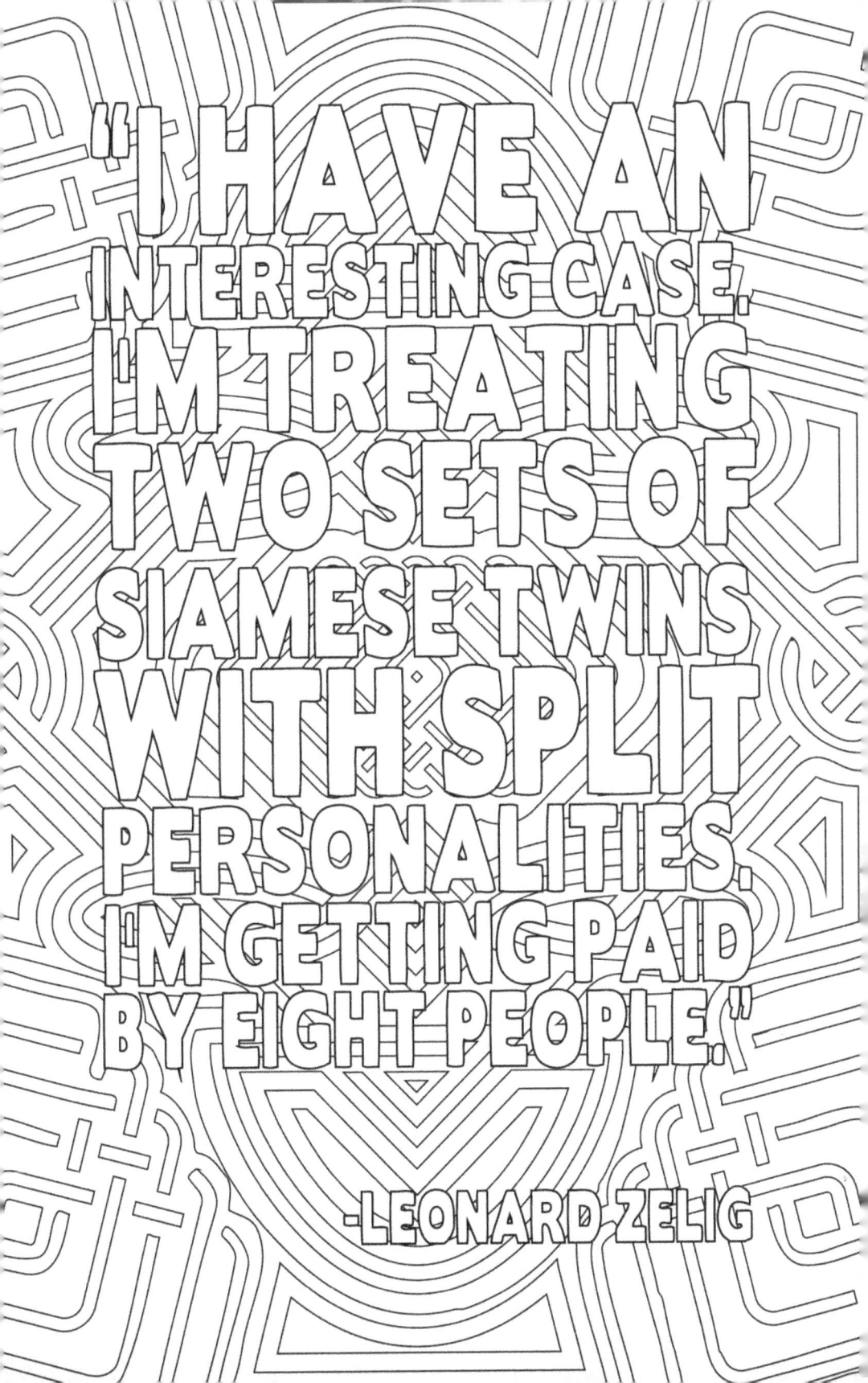

"I HAVE AN INTERESTING CASE. I'M TREATING TWO SETS OF SIAMESE TWINS WITH SPLIT PERSONALITIES. I'M GETTING PAID BY EIGHT PEOPLE."

-LEONARD ZELIG

"DON'T EVER HIT YOUR MOTHER WITH A SHOVEL. IT LEAVES A DULL IMPRESSION ON HER MIND."

-BUTCH CASSSIDY

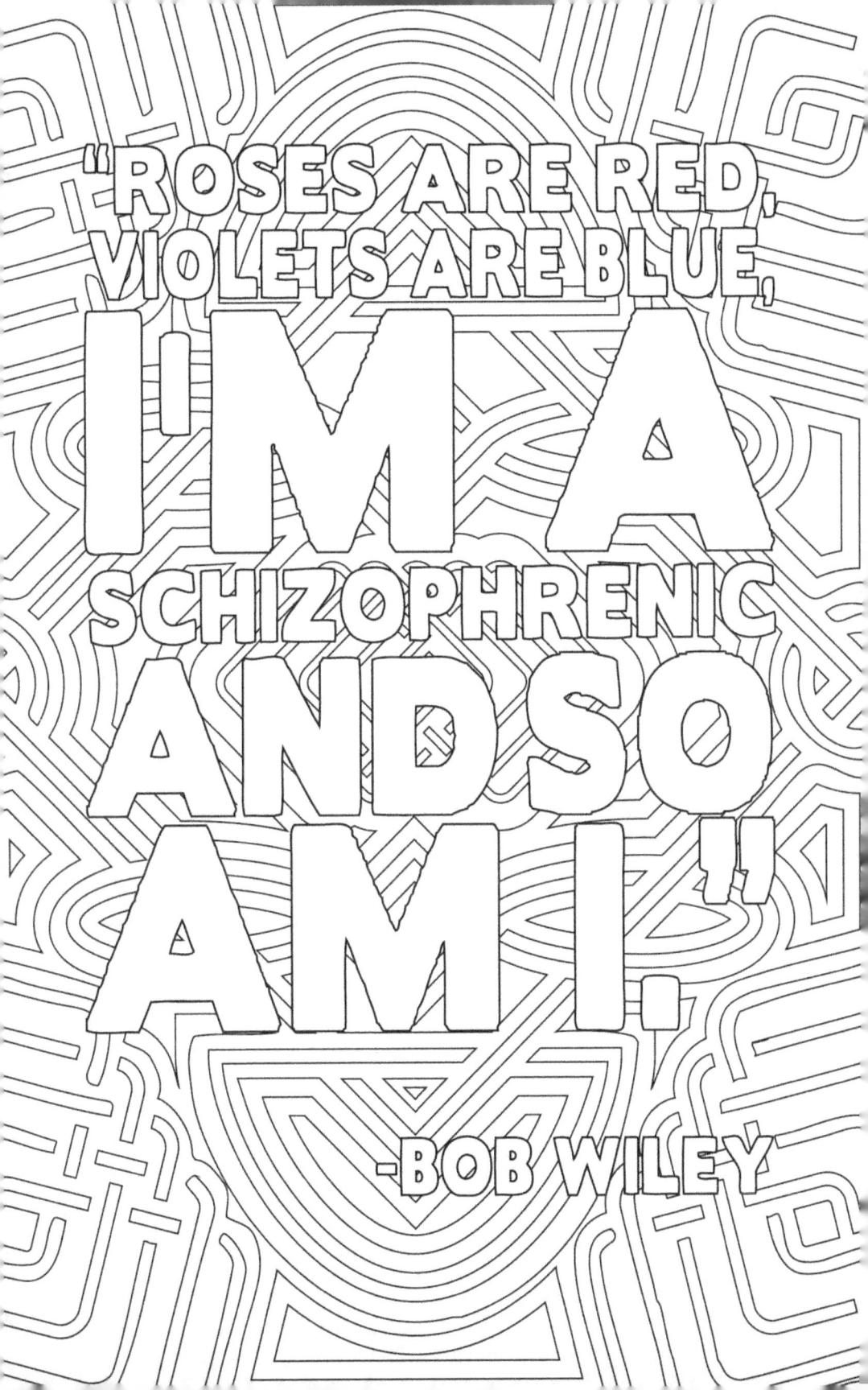

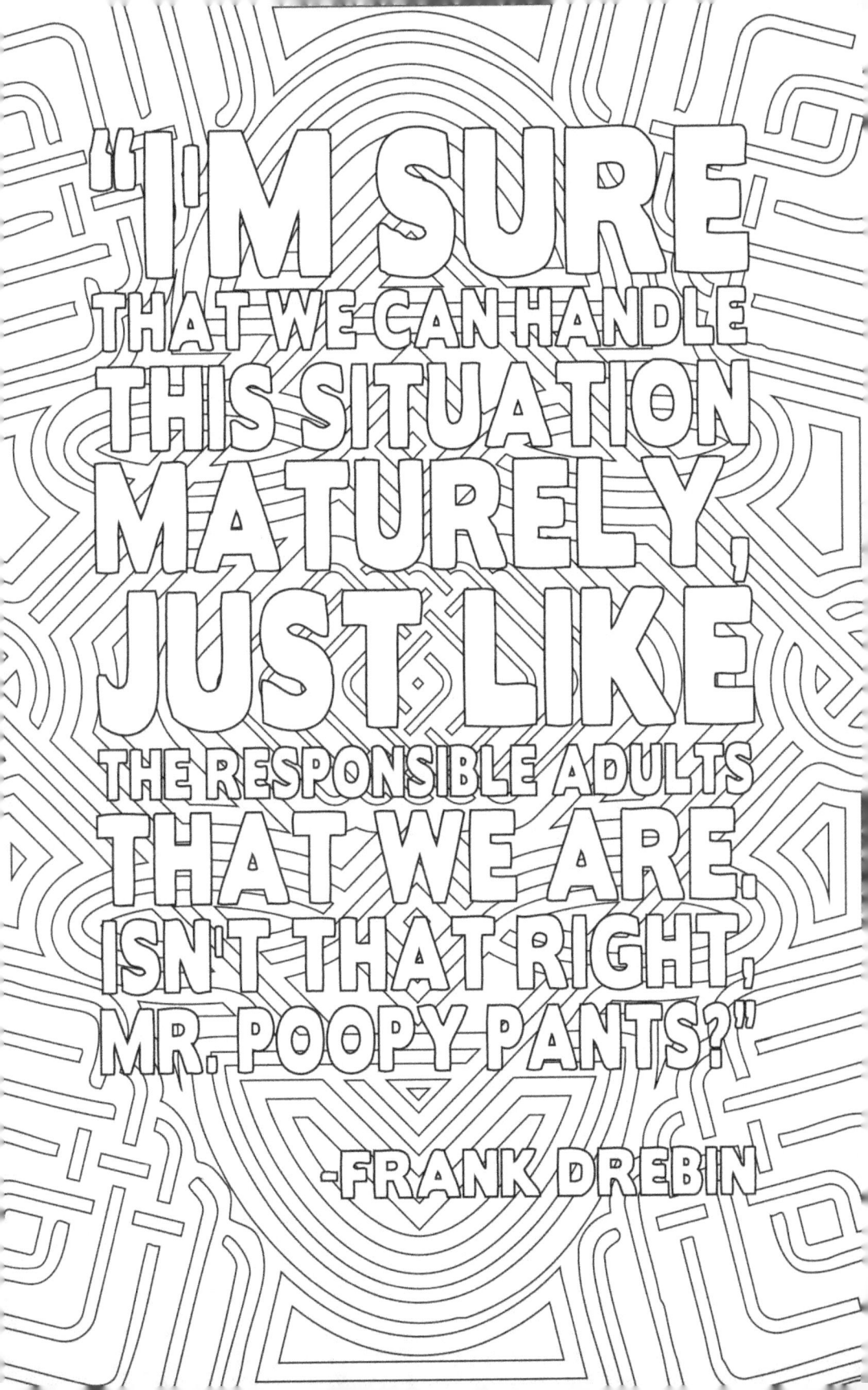

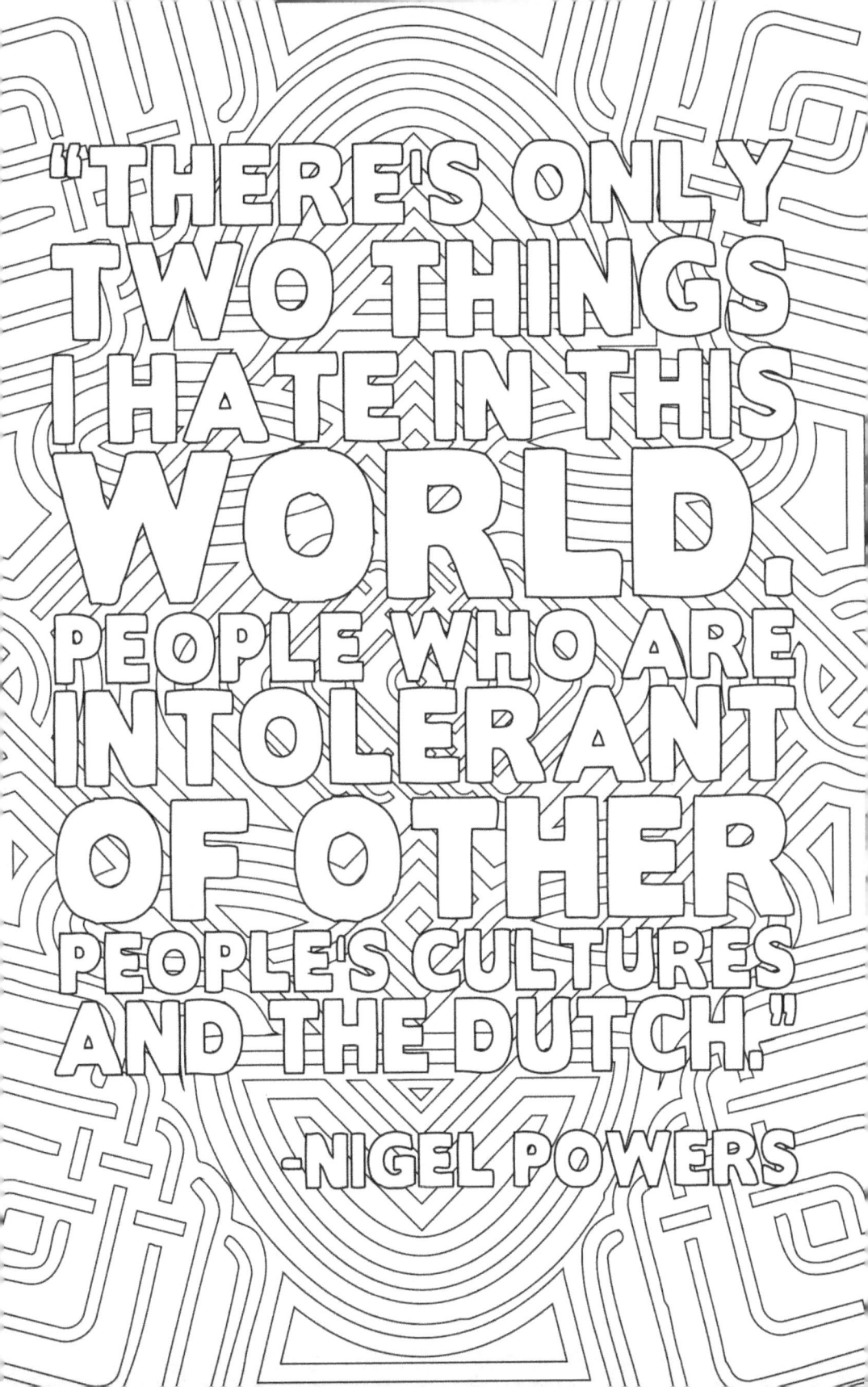

"YOU KNOW WHAT'S MORE DESTRUCTIVE THAN A NUCLEAR BOMB? WORDS" "..."

-KIM JONG UN

"LIFE DOES NOT STOP AND START AT YOUR CONVENIENCE, YOU MISERABLE PIECE OF SHIT!"

-WALTER

"YOU MET ME AT A VERY STRANGE TIME IN MY LIFE."

-NARRATOR

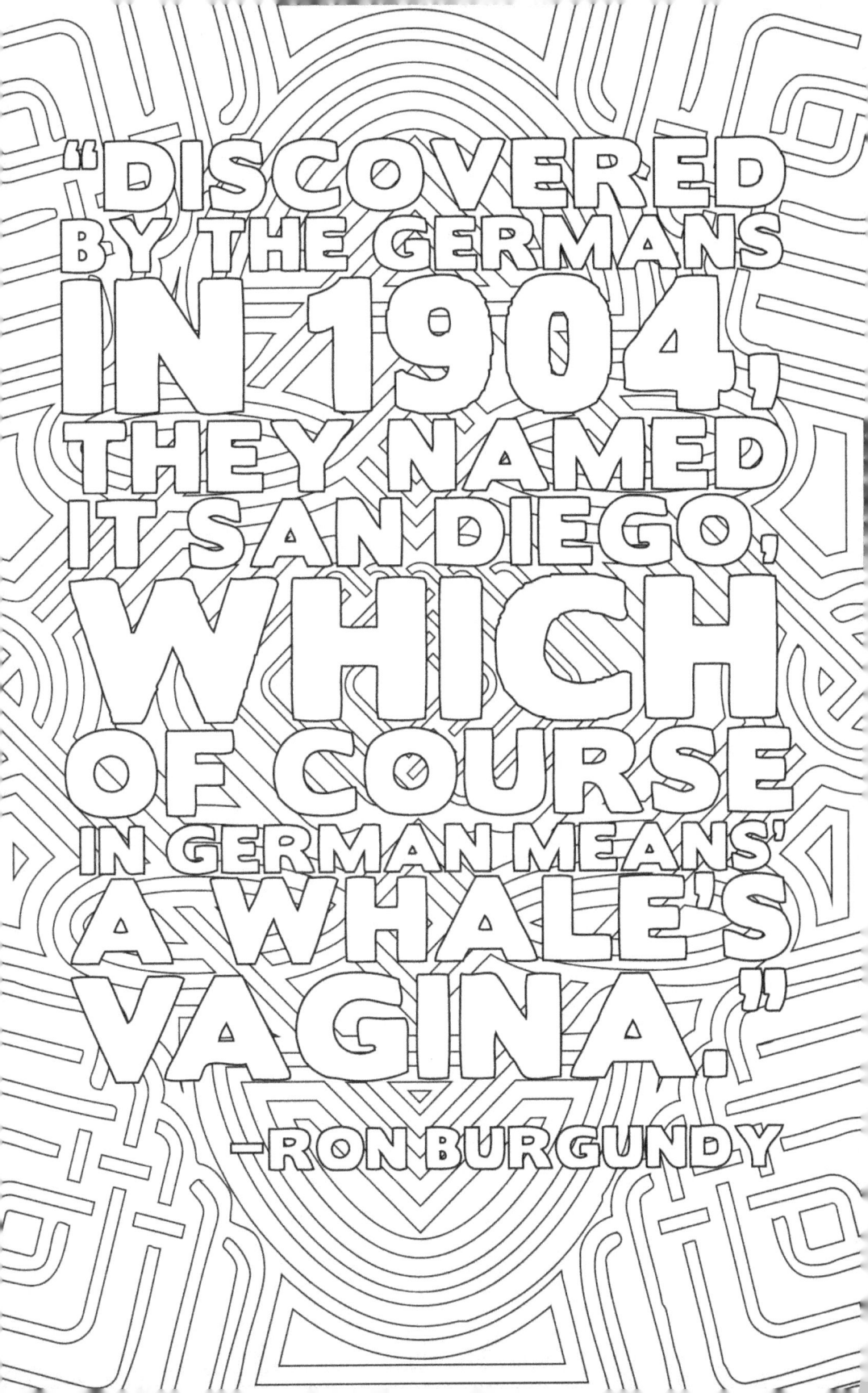

"COME OUT TO THE COAST, WE'LL GET TOGETHER, HAVE A FEW LAUGHS..."

-JOHN MCCLANE

"I DON'T DATE THESE GIRLS BECAUSE THEY'RE WELL-READ. I GAVE ONE OF THEM A COPY OF "FAREWELL TO ARMS". SHE THOUGHT IT WAS A DIET BOOK."

-HENRY FINE

THE END?

R J DUNCAN MAKES HIS LIVING WRITING SILLY BOOKS LIKE THIS ONE AND MAYBE SOMETHING A BIT MORE SERIOUS FROM TIME TO TIME. IF YOU ENJOYED THIS BOOK, CHECK OUT ALL THE OTHER ONES,

OR

IF YOU WOULD LIKE DUNCAN TO MAKE A BOOK *JUST FOR YOU* , WITH YOU PICKING ALL OF THE CONTENT, GET IN TOUCH:

www.RJDUNCANBOOKS.com

BECAUSE WHO THE HELL DOESN'T WANT A BOOK MADE FOR THEIR BIRTHDAY, BACHELOR'S PARTY, FAMILY GATHERING, FLAG DAY?

For more,
follow me on:

 Duncan Books

 @robduncanbooks

 @DuncanBooks_Rob

 Rob Duncan Books

ISBN 9781544109541

90000 >

9 781544 109541